THE ULTIMATE GUIDE BOOK FOR ONLINE AND OFFLINE COACHING BUSINESS OWNERS OF INDIA

MAKE MILLION DOLLAR COACHING BUSINESS

THRIVE IN ANY ECONOMY, AND BUILD BIG BRAND THAT YOU DREAM

THE ULTIMATE GUIDE BOOK FOR ONLINE AND OFFLINE COACHING BUSINESS OWNERS OF INDIA

MAKE MILLION DOLLAR COACHING BUSINESS

THRIVE IN ANY ECONOMY, AND BUILD BIG BRAND THAT YOU DREAM

ATUL JAIN

Worldwide Published by
Pendown Press

PENDOWN PRESS LLP

An ISO 9001 & ISO 14001 Certified Co.

Regd. Office 3767A, Kanhaiya Nagar,
Tri Nagar, Delhi-110035
Ph.: 8180886000, 9650072927, 8595249536
E-mail: info@pendownpress.com
Branch Office 1A/2A, 20, Hari Sadan, Ansari Road,
Daryaganj, New Delhi-110002
Ph.: 011-45794768
Website: PendownPress.com

First Edition: 2023
Price: ₹399/-
ISBN: 978-93-5554-688-3

LayoutAnd Cover Designed by Pendown Graphics Team
PrintedAnd Bound in India by Thomson Press India Ltd.

Contents

About The Book

By writing a book for educators who want to grow online or who are unsure about where to start, I aim to empower and inspire these dedicated educators on their digital journey. I want to provide practical guidance, valuable insights, and action-taking strategies that will allow educators to overcome the challenges they face in the online world.

This book is also for those who want to teach and impact students on both online and offline platforms. As an educator, you have the skills to teach offline and Covid-19 taught us to adapt to the online model too. Technically, by following a hybrid approach, educators can completely change their game. Through online teaching, educators can reach a wider audience and impact on a mass scale. Offline teaching, on the other hand, allows for personalized interaction and attention which is required for delivering the much-needed results.

By combining both platforms, educators can create a power-packed teaching profession that can shield them from any possible challenges in the future.

About The Author

Carrying a unique blend of knowledge in the field of Software Engineering and Management in Marketing, Atul Jain is on a mission to impact the lives of 10000 educators and 20 lacs students. Having a brief but effective experience of 7 years in the ed-tech industry, Atul has helped hundreds of educators setup an efficient system of teaching in both offline & online world.

How To Use This Book

This book is designed in such a way that anybody from a beginner to a pro-level educator can use the concepts explained in the chapters ahead. The *TT Framework* is a unique method that needs to be followed in a practical way. We will learn more about this in the coming pages.

Follow the *TT Framework* step-by-step and do not hesitate to refer to it whenever you need clarification or guidance. By utilizing this book as a roadmap, you can maximize its value and benefit from the wealth of knowledge it offers, ultimately enhancing your understanding and proficiency in the subject matter.

Acknowledgement

I am immensely grateful to all the wonderful customers with whom I have got a chance to work with. Your trust in my expertise and the opportunity to serve you in the development of a Coaching Institute has been truly rewarding. Your dedication to education and commitment to empowering students have inspired me to share my knowledge and experiences in this book. Your support has been the driving force behind my efforts, and I extend my heartfelt appreciation for your continued belief in my work.

I express my deepest gratitude to my Marketing Guru and mentor, Mr. Akshar Yadav. Your mentorship, guidance, and invaluable insights have been pivotal in shaping my understanding of marketing principles and strategies. Your unwavering support, encouragement, and belief in my potential have motivated me to take on this ambitious venture of writing a book. I am immensely grateful for your generosity in sharing The Get Overbooked framework and The 13 Principles of Marketing, which had a transformative impact on my professional growth.

To my beloved family, words cannot express the depth of my gratitude for your unswerving support and encouragement throughout my journey of writing this book, before and even beyond that.

Your love, understanding, and sacrifices have been the bedrock of my strength and determination. Your belief in my abilities, countless hours spent providing feedback and encouragement, and the sacrifices you have made along the way have made this accomplishment possible. Thank you for standing by me and for being my pillar of strength.

With deep appreciation and gratitude,

Atul Jain

Creator of TT Framework
The Ultimate Guidebook to a Successful Coaching Profession

Chapter 1

The Hard Truths

Running a coaching institute is a fulfilling yet demanding aspiration that requires immense dedication and a passion for education. As an educator, when coaching the students, you take up a noble mission to guide and shape the futures of aspiring students and India as a whole. However, it is essential to recognize that this journey is filled with challenges.

1. **Curriculum:** One of the major challenges is designing and implementing a curriculum that meets the evolving needs and expectations of students. The competitive exam ecosystem is constantly evolving, with new subjects, technologies, and teaching methodologies emerging regularly. Keeping up with these changes, staying ahead, and tailoring the curriculum to align with the demands of standardized exams and competitive assessments can be a daunting task.

2. **Personalized attention:** Coaching institute owners also face the challenge of managing a diverse set of students with varying learning styles, abilities, and ambitions, Each student comes with unique strengths, weaknesses, and academic goals, and they silently demand

personalized teaching approaches. Striking the right balance between group teaching and one-to-one support, while maintaining high academic standards, can be demanding.

3. **Money matters:** Furthermore, financial management is a critical concern for coaching institute owners. Balancing operational expenses, faculty salaries, infrastructure development, and marketing efforts while ensuring affordability for students can pose considerable financial challenges. Budgeting, cost optimization, and exploring alternative revenue streams become essential to sustain and grow the coaching institute.

4. **Fierce Competition:** Lastly, the coaching industry has witnessed a remarkable increase in competition, due to the growth of both online and offline teaching environments. Covid-19 taught us a lot of things, and one major lesson we learned was that many educators adopted a more virtual way of teaching. Gradually, it helped them reach a wider base of students, with numerous online coaching providers offering comprehensive curricula, mock tests, and interactive learning experiences at more affordable costs. This allows students to have various options to choose from, irrespective of geographical limitations. Consequently, this has led to increased competition among online as well as offline coaching platforms.

Despite these challenges, coaching institute owners who maintain consistency and embrace innovation can establish an environment conducive to academic excellence and empower students to achieve their goals.

By addressing these obstacles head-on with technology and leveraging their passion for education, coaching institute owners can make a lasting impact on the lives of countless students, shaping future generations.

Covid-19 and the Rise of Online Education

The COVID-19 pandemic has highlighted the immense potential of coaching institutes, particularly in the digital realm.

Real-life examples such as Unacademy, Physics Wallah, and Khan Sir exemplify the transformative impact of coaching institutes in the post-pandemic era.

Unacademy, a popular online learning platform, offers a wide array of courses taught by experienced educators across various subjects and competitive exams like NEET, JEE, UPSC, etc. Their interactive live classes, comprehensive study materials, and doubt-solving sessions have helped countless students achieve academic success.

Physics Wallah, founded by Alakh Pandey on YouTube in 2016, has gained widespread recognition across the country for its free educational videos and online coaching. After 2020, Alakh, along with his team of educators and app developers, started offering a unique teaching style at immensely affordable rates. Students from all financial backgrounds began learning through the app, creating thousands of successful case students across the country. The company was valued at USD $1 Billion in 2022, making it an ed-tech unicorn of India. Now, they are opening various offline institutes named VIDYAPEETH in many cities.

Nobody knew Khan Sir a few years back. During that time, he was a common man just like us. But something happened during the year 2020. By consistently following his passion for teaching and utilizing free online platforms to post content, along with the right tech equipment, he became an online sensation. Today, he teaches on both online and offline platforms, with each batch's strength exceeding 2 lakh students in the online platform and over 20,000 students in the offline platform.

The examples shared above are growing by leaps and bounds by opting a hybrid curriculum. I personally believe that the hybrid way of teaching, i.e., having a strong presence in both online and offline platforms, is the way to go from here. All those educators who adopt this change will survive because change is the only thing you can count on.

The Power of Online teaching – Educator's Point of view

Teaching online brings a wide range of benefits that have revolutionized the field of education. Online education enables learners to access educational resources and interact with instructors regardless of their geographical location. It provides flexibility in terms of scheduling, allowing students to learn at their own pace. Additionally, online teaching promotes collaboration, enhances digital literacy, and offers a wealth of multimedia resources. Overall, teaching online offers a dynamic and inclusive learning environment that empowers students and educators alike.

Let Me Explain

1. **Expanded Reach:** By embracing online teaching, coaching institutes can go beyond geographical limitations and reach students beyond their local area. This opens up a vast market of potential learners, allowing institutes to attract students from different cities, regions, or even countries. It expands the institute's reach and potential student base, leading to increased enrollment and revenue opportunities.

2. **Cost Savings:** Online teaching can be cost-effective for coaching institutes. They can significantly reduce expenses associated with maintaining physical infrastructure, such as rent, utilities, and maintenance. Additionally, travel costs for instructors and students are eliminated, saving both time and money. These cost savings can be reinvested in improving the quality of education or expanding course offerings.

3. **Enhanced Teaching Resources:** Online teaching enables coaching institutes to utilize a variety of digital tools and resources to enhance the learning experience. They can integrate multimedia content, such as videos, simulations, and interactive quizzes, to make the classes more engaging and interactive. Institutes can also leverage learning management systems (LMS) or Android-based applications to organize and distribute course materials, track student progress, and provide additional study resources.

4. **Scalability and Standardization:** Online teaching offers scalability for coaching institutes. They can easily replicate and distribute standardized course content to a larger number of students. This ensures consistent delivery of high-quality instruction, regardless of the number of students enrolled. Coaching institutes can maintain a standardized curriculum, assessment methods, and teaching methodologies, ensuring a uniform learning experience across different cohorts.

The Power of Online Teaching – Student's Point of View

From a student's point of view, the power of online learning is immense. It opens a world of opportunities and possibilities. Online learning also instills independence and self-discipline, as students must take responsibility for their learning journey. The power of online learning lies in its ability to empower students with knowledge, skills, and opportunities that can shape their futures and unlock their full potential.

Let Me Explain

1. **Accessibility and Flexibility:** Online platforms offer students the opportunity to choose their preferred educator from anywhere in India. This flexibility allows students to learn from the comfort of their own homes or any geographical location that suits them best. This accessibility and flexibility can save both time and money.

2. **Cost Savings:** Online learning platforms often provide more affordable options compared to traditional educational institutions. Since these students rely on their parents for financial support, online courses can be a cost-effective alternative. They eliminate the need for expenses such as transportation, accommodation, and other associated costs. Additionally, many online platforms offer free or low-cost educational resources, reducing the financial burden on students and their families.

The difficulty of setting up a h   id model

Being an educator and transitioning/expanding to an online platform is a complex process that only looks achievable on the surface level.

While it may appear effortless, the reality is that going online poses numerous challenges for educators. They must adapt to new teaching methodologies, navigate unfamiliar technology, and develop effective strategies for engaging students in a virtual environment.

Additionally, blending both traditional and online education requires careful planning, smart organization of resources, and constant troubleshooting to ensure the smooth delivery of content.

It demands a significant investment of time, effort, and continuous learning to master the complexities of online teaching, making it a more challenging process than it may initially seem.

With this in mind, it is time to unravel the fastest and most proven method to transition and thrive online.

This method is a blend of both platforms, thus creating an ideal way to super-strengthen your coaching institute.

The Framework is a close analysis of the lives of more than 100 educators and their approach before and after Covid. Learning this framework will help you cover your journey of 5 years in just 1 year.

Having said that, let us explore the *TT Framework*

Chapter 2

Story of Jayant

Jayant, a 31-year-old educator from Jaipur, had dedicated four years of his life to teaching offline. He had built a reputation as an exceptional teacher, known for his commitment and passion for his students' success. His coaching institute was a place where young minds blossomed, and dreams were nurtured.

However, when the COVID-19 pandemic struck, everything came crashing down. Schools and coaching centers were forced to close their doors indefinitely, and Jayant's world turned upside down. The sudden halt to his offline teaching left him feeling lost and uncertain about the future.

Jayant had always enjoyed face-to-face interactions with his students. He loved seeing their enthusiasm and curiosity first hand, and he valued the personal connection he had built with each one of them. The transition to online teaching was a difficult medicine to swallow. The absence of physical presence and limited interaction left him feeling disconnected and disheartened.

As he transitioned to the online realm, Jayant realized that competition had become fiercer than ever before. Established coaching centers quickly adapted and created impressive online portals, while other individual tutors flooded the internet with their offerings to capture students. Jayant struggled to gain visibility in the saturated market, as students were bombarded with numerous offers and exciting promises from other educators.

Day after day, Jayant dedicated himself to refining his online teaching skills, improving his content, and engaging with his students through virtual platforms. He spent countless hours developing innovative lesson plans and adapting his teaching methods to suit the online environment. Despite his best efforts, the constant struggle to compete with both offline and online competitors began taking a toll on him emotionally.

"Jayant's coaching business faced significant setbacks. Many of his students, who were used to the traditional classroom experience, found it challenging to adapt to the new online format. Some lost interest, while others sought alternative options that seemed more appealing or convenient. Jayant watched helplessly as the number of students enrolling in his classes reduced, and his once-thriving coaching institute became a shadow of its former self.

The financial pain grew heavier with each passing day. Jayant had invested a big chunk of his savings into marketing just before Covid, but unfortunately, the returns were very poor. The rents, salaries, and other fixed costs and the pressure to keep his business afloat weighed heavily on his shoulders.

Loneliness began to creep into Jayant's life. The absence of daily interactions with students and colleagues left him feeling isolated. The joy he once derived from teaching was replaced by a sense of sadness and hopelessness. The once vibrant and enthusiastic educator now found himself questioning his purpose and passion.

Despite facing numerous hardships, Jayant was determined not to give up. Drawing strength from the support of his family and close friends, they encouraged him to persevere and find new ways to tackle the challenges. With a new found determination, Jayant proactively reached out to his existing students and their parents, seeking their feedback and suggestions to make improvement.

Gradually, Jayant began to see a glimmer of hope. The positive responses and testimonials from his loyal students reminded him of his true worth as an educator. He realized that his impact on their lives extended beyond the physical walls of his institute. Their success stories and gratitude became his driving force to continue pushing forward.

Jayant successfully survived the storm of the COVID-19 pandemic for two long years. As the world slowly regained a normal life, the coaching industry had undergone a significant transformation. With the introduction of hybrid learning, big companies had entered the arena, offering their own curriculum and resources. This new teaching format brought a huge wave of competition that Jayant had never experienced before.

Over time, the days transformed into weeks, and the weeks into months, leading Jayant to embark on a path of self-improvement. He actively participated in seminars, webinars, and workshops, dedicating himself to enhancing his hybrid teaching skills and staying updated with the latest advancements in educational technology.

In the latest seminar held in Delhi, Jayant experienced something truly exceptional and empowering – a seminar that was unlike any other, filled with hope and promise..

Aman, the guest speaker for the seminar, explained the *TT Framework* and its magical potential in developing a Covid-proof hybrid coaching, while Jayant listened patiently.

As soon as the seminar was over, Jayant rushed to Aman, who was about to take a seat after a 3-hour long session. Aman was very happy to meet Jayant, as he could see a flow of passion in the conversation with him. Aman had to catch a flight, so he gave his e-Card to Jayant and told him to connect after 2 days to learn more about the *TT Framework*.

Chapter 3

Journey to the East

As Jayant waited in the reception area of Aman's office, he observed the bustling environment around him. The office seemed busy, with people focused on their work and engaged in discussions. Jayant took a seat and patiently awaited Aman's arrival. After traveling 24 hours by train and directly reaching Aman's office in Kolkata, Jayant was a bit tired.

Meanwhile, Aman was engaged in a Zoom call with another educator who was onboarded three months ago. They were discussing the progress of the framework that Jayant was eager to learn about.

While Jayant waited, he took the opportunity to observe the office surroundings and engage in small talk with some of the employees. He hoped that once Aman finished his call, he would get a chance to discuss the Framework and learn more about its application in his industry.

Time passed, and eventually, Aman's Zoom call came to an end. He wrapped up his conversation, bid farewell to the educator, and made his way to the reception area where he found Jayant. Aman greeted Jayant with a warm smile and invited him to his room, ready to share his knowledge and insights about the *TT Framework*.

Chapter 4

TT Framework

The TT (Technique and Technology) Framework is an innovative approach that combines the use of techniques and technology to accelerate online growth and establish a hybrid curriculum. It aims to leverage the benefits of both traditional teaching techniques and online technological advancements to create an effective and engaging learning experience.

Aman started to explain the entire framework and told Jayant to imagine himself at the base camp of the snowy peaks of Mount Everest. Aman explained that climbing Everest symbolized establishing a fully functional hybrid coaching institute, where reaching the top represented success. Aman emphasized that just as conquering Everest required both technique and the right tools, creating a successful coaching institute demanded a combination of effective technique and cutting-edge technology.

Chapter 5

Technique

One common mistake people make when growing an online teaching environment is randomly choosing teaching methods without any scientific basis. Without a strategic approach, you risk wasting time and effort on ineffective techniques. By neglecting to understand your target audience, ignoring marketing principles, or failing to adapt to online learning environments, you miss out on opportunities for meaningful engagement and growth. It is essential to take a thoughtful and research-based approach to ensure fruitful efforts.

Jayant was keenly listening and taking down notes to Aman's analogy.

Aman then showed this picture to Jayant and asked him,

'What do you observe?'

"Heavy snow," replied Jayant.

'Correct', said Aman, and then asked him again,

'What do you think about these people?'

'That they are all following a common path', said Jayant.

'Exactly!!' roared Aman."

"The technique is basically the path that needs to be followed by an educator. This path is known to very few and they are one of the most successful educators in their domain" explained Aman.

The path is divided into 4 parts

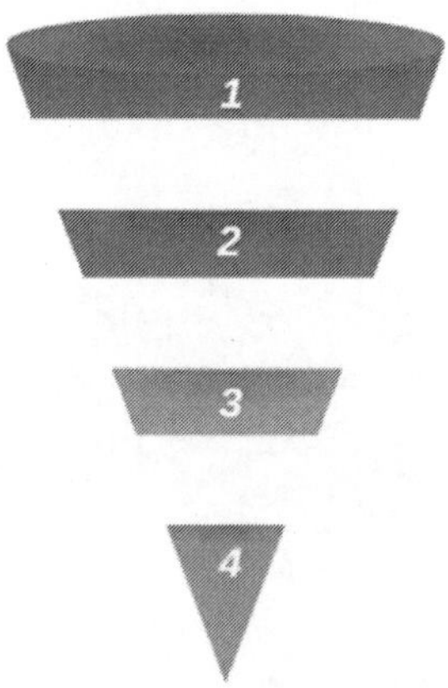

Let us understand each part one by one

1) Maximize student leads

Generating leads from various sources is a well-known practice among educators. Educators are aware of the diverse channels available for lead generation, including traditional methods like referrals, word-of-mouth, and public hoardings as well as digital strategies such as social media marketing, and search engine optimization. By utilizing these known lead generation sources, educators can enhance their visibility, engage with a wider audience, and ultimately speed up student inquiry in their educational institutions.

Each method has its pros and cons. None of them can be called poor, but only a few are effective. If we can deeply understand 1 or 2 media of lead generation, it is going to change the game. The problem is that we do not have proper knowledge about the technique of generating leads. Whatever we have done till now is mainly through word-of-mouth-based marketing.

YouTube as a platform is a super-effective method of generating leads. If used wisely, an educator does not need any other platform. Today 82% of students who want to learn anything are on YouTube between age 10-24.

"But I already know about YouTube, and I have a channel for the past 1 year," said Jayant.

"Okay but have you been properly utilizing your YouTube channel? Do you know the science behind what is working and what is not working on YouTube?" asked Aman.

"No," said Jayant softly.

As one of the largest social media platforms, YouTube offers a vast audience and the opportunity to showcase your talent, establish credibility by giving valuable content and attract potential students. Here is an explanation and introduction to using YouTube for lead generation in the education industry:

1. **Content Creation:** Educators and coaching institutes can create videos that provide valuable educational content, tutorials, tips, and insights in their respective fields. These videos should be designed to engage viewers and offer practical knowledge or assistance. By consistently uploading high-quality content, you can establish yourself or your institute as a thought leader in the industry.

2. **Visibility:** YouTube is the second-largest search engine after Google, which means your videos can be visible to anybody across the world without any cost. By incorporating relevant keywords in video titles, descriptions, and hashtags, you can increase the chances of your videos being discovered by students searching for content on which you have already made videos on.

3. **Call-to-Action (CTA):** To generate leads, it's important to include a CTA in your videos. This can be a verbal mention or a text overlay that encourages viewers to

take action. For example, you can ask them to call on a particular number to understand more about the concepts on which you have created videos.

4. **Branding and Professionalism:** Maintain a consistent brand image across your YouTube channel by using professional graphics, logos, and channel art. Ensure your videos have high production quality, good lighting, and clear audio. A visually appealing and well-branded channel can help establish trust and attract potential students or clients.

Assuming you know the basics of YouTube then you need to follow the things that I have mentioned below. These points will help you earn subscribers faster thus generating more leads.

1. **Complete Audience Clarity:** By understanding the audience's needs, preferences, and learning styles, educators can tailor their videos to ensure maximum views. As an educator, you must ask questions to your students about what content they are constantly searching for on the internet. And when you have clarity, you create content around that and give it some time. The biggest problem is that, as educators, we often make content based on what we think our audience wants. This is actually not the right approach.

2. **Unique and Relatable YouTube videos:** Unique videos can stand out from the jungle of videos, capturing students' attention and sparking their curiosity. This can be achieved by presenting information in a creative and visually appealing way, using animations, storytelling techniques, or incorporating real-life examples. Relatable videos, on the other hand, establish a connection between the educator and the students by addressing their concerns, challenges, and interests. Educators can create relatable content by discussing relevant topics, sharing personal experiences, or addressing common misconceptions. To attract views, create magnetic thumbnails that are visually enticing and represent the essence of your video content.

3. **Thumbnails:** The science of thumbnails starts with emotions. The main purpose of thumbnails is to trigger emotions compelling viewers to click on the video. There are 4 emotions, namely happiness, fear, hope, and curiosity, any of which must be triggered while making a thumbnail. No matter how powerful your video is, If your thumbnail is poor, you will never get views.

4. **Channel Description & Channel Trailer:** From an educator's perspective, channel description serves as a concise introduction, allowing educators to showcase their qualifications and the educational content they offer. By providing this information, educators can

establish credibility and trust with potential learners, enticing them to explore the content further. On the other hand, a channel trailer serves as a fascinating preview, offering a glimpse into the educational experience provided by the channel.

5. **Video title, hashtags, and video descrip**tion: A well-crafted title helps with search engine optimization (SEO) and increases the chances of your video appearing in relevant search results. It also sets the viewer's expectations and entices them to click and watch the video. Hashtags are keywords or phrases preceded by the '#' symbol that categorizes and organizes content on YouTube. Including relevant hashtags in your video description or title can help increase discoverability and reach a wider audience. It allows viewers interested in specific topics to find your content more easily. Video descriptions should be informative, engaging, and aligned with your target audience's needs and interests. Providing valuable and well-structured descriptions establishes your expertise and encourages viewers to subscribe and continue watching your videos.

Once you keep doing 1 to 5 consistently, you will gradually see a healthy rise in your channel and start leveraging leads from your channel.

"Feeling hungry?" Asked Aman

"Yes sir," said Jayant

"Let's have food and then continue!" said Aman

2) Create a Strong Online foundation

It was late in the evening, and both of them had finished their dinner.

"Shall we continue?" Asked Aman

"Certainly!!" said Jayant

"Let's Go then" replied Aman

An online foundation refers to the digital presence of an educator and the visibility of individuals, organizations, or brands on the internet. It can be of various forms such as websites, landing pages, mobile applications, and portals that facilitate interaction, engagement, and the dissemination of information or services.

Once the lead is generated, the student should swiftly move from YouTube to your online platform where he/she can access more intriguing information about just you and your institute.

Let me explain a few fundamental but powerful online platforms that can effectively showcase you as an authority in front of unaware students and what they should comprise.

Website:

A website serves as a virtual representation and information hub for educators and coaching institute owners. It must exhibit the

a. Institute's offerings,

b. Faculty profiles,

c. Teaching methodologies,

d. Course details,

e. Testimonials, past results & performances, and

f. Exciting Offers which students cannot control

g. Contact information.

Additionally, a website can offer an array of resources, such as study materials, practice tests, or online courses, catering to the specific requirements of educators and coaching institute owners.

Landing Page:

A landing page serves as a single web page strategically designed to capture the attention of students and prompt them to take a desired action. For educators and coaching institute owners, a landing page can be used to promote a specific course, workshop, or training program. It should include

a. Compelling content,

b. Highlights of the program's benefits,

- **c.** Testimonials from successful participants, and
- **d.** A clear call-to-action to encourage interested individuals to enroll or learn more.

Android Application:

An Android application customized for educators and coaching institute owners can provide convenient access to a plethora of resources and tools directly on their mobile devices. This app may include features such as

- **a.** Lesson planning tools,
- **b.** Student management systems,
- **c.** Performance analytics,
- **d.** Communication methods, and
- **e.** Updates on the latest teaching methodologies and educational trends.

Additionally, it can provide a platform for networking and collaboration among educators and institute owners.

Portal:

A portal represents a comprehensive web-based platform that offers a range of resources, services, and utilities for educators and coaching institute owners. It can serve as a centralized hub for course management, student data tracking, online assessments, community forums, professional development materials, and administrative functions. A portal can foster collaboration, facilitate knowledge sharing, and support the growth and development of educators and coaching institute owners.

The ultimate agenda of having an online portal is to drive students towards your demo sessions. Your portal should lead to a registration form where students can enroll for your demo session. Whenever a demo session begins, you can notify all registered students. This is the new way of doing targeted marketing.

During your demo session give it your 100%. Students expect comprehensive coverage and clarity of the topic too. Make sure you choose those topics which can be covered in demo sessions. Always try to build trust by interacting with them, addressing their questions or queries post the session.

Every teacher possesses a distinct teaching style. And a student always correlates with a teacher who can touch the student's emotions. Some teachers are funny while some are motivating. Always follow your style as it makes you unique from the world and that is the reason why students will ultimately join your class.

And as we approach the end, it is always about an offer. Make them an offer that they simply cannot refuse like a limited-time coupon or a special code for the first admission, so on and so forth. This will excite some of the students to join you. You cannot be there to convince them to join you. It can only be done through marketing and this method of offering attractive deals is a part of the marketing.

3) Mega online batch

Once the demo sessions are over, your CTA is to call them to your next platform which is the mega online batch. Keep the online batch open to a maximum number of students. The commitment here is to provide valuable information and knowledge at a fairly lower cost.

If you are charging 2000 per subject in the traditional coaching method, charge 500 here. If you are charging 20000, charge 4000 here. The idea is simple.

Follow the concept followed by famous teachers like Alakh Pandey and Khan sir. This is the game.

Since the energy needed to teach 5 students online is the same as teaching 50 students online and there is no barrier of physical infrastructure, it is advisable to maximize students here. The only thing you need to ensure is not reducing the quality of teaching and curriculum as a whole. You must deliver what you promised during the initial level.

You must also be smart enough to handle technology as students start increasing. We can discuss that some other day.

4) Advanced offline batche

The biggest challenge in the industry which is faced by 95% of educators is that they never choose, instead the students choose them. Students choose based on results, based on fees, based on faculty, etc. If, as an educator, you are not building your institute in such a way that allows you to choose the right students, not the other way around, then nothing will happen.

A skilled teacher never gets chosen but rather chooses his students.

In this way, the overall results of that educator naturally goes higher.

You can also take hybrid classes (offline and online) at the same time. You can create a curriculum where online students can have the opportunity for doubt solving sessions and live lectures both.

Chapter 6

This Concludes 4 Parts of Techniques

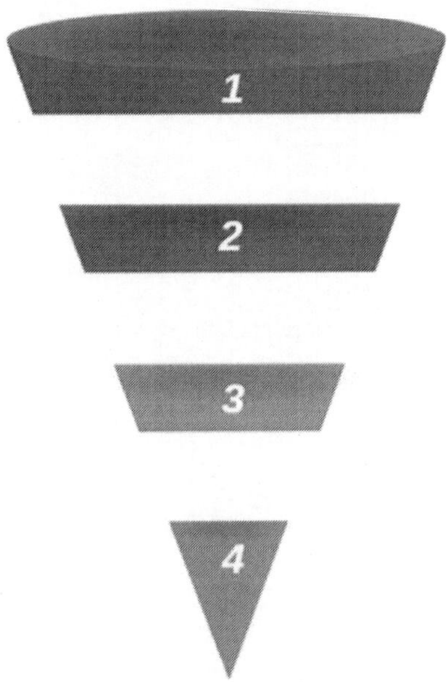

Analogy

Aman then gave an analogy where he described how the future of coaching education will move towards a more hybrid approach.

He created 2 scenarios:

Scenario 1

In this scenario, the educator adopts a flexible and diverse approach to teaching.

They offer two types of classes:

1. Online classes with a fee of 18,000 rupees and a student strength of 500, and
2. Advanced Offline classes with a fee of 50,000 rupees and 80 students to be handpicked by the educator's choice from the offline batch of 500 students. The total revenue generated from both types of classes is 1.3 crores.

Scenario 2

In this scenario, the educator is conducting three offline batches with a total strength of 200 students. Each student pays a fee of 40,000 rupees, resulting in a total revenue of 80 lakhs. However, there are certain limitations to this approach.

Losses in Scenario 2

Limited Reach: By exclusively conducting offline classes, the educator's reach is restricted to a local or specific geographical area. This limits the potential student base and prevents the educator from reaching a larger audience.

Fixed Time and Space Constraints

Offline batches require physical classrooms, which may have limitations on capacity. Moreover, the educator needs to adhere to a fixed schedule for each batch, making it difficult to accommodate students who may have other commitments or prefer different time slots.

Higher Fees

While the educator charges a higher fee per student in Scenario 1, the limited number of students and the constraints of offline classes prevent them from maximizing their revenue potential.

Jayant thoroughly explained his understanding to Aman between the two scenarios and arrive to the following conclusion:

Increased Revenue

Scenario 1 generates significantly higher revenue (1.3 crores) compared to Scenario 2 (80 lakhs). By diversifying the teaching methods and reaching out to both online and offline students, educators expand their potential market and capture a larger audience.

Enhanced Reach and Flexibility

With online classes in Scenario 1, the educator attracts a broader range of students from different locations. Online classes eliminate the constraints of physical space and provide flexible schedules, accommodating students' preferences and availability.

Lower Fees for Online Classes

Although the fee per student is lower for online classes (18,000 rupees) compared to offline classes (50,000 rupees), the increased student count in online classes compensates for the lower fee, resulting in higher overall revenue.

In summary, Scenario 1 offers significant advantages over Scenario 2. The educator in Scenario 1 expands their reach, enjoys more flexibility, and generates substantially higher revenue by adopting a combination of online and offline classes. The losses incurred in Scenario 2 due to limited reach, fixed constraints, and higher fees can be mitigated in Scenario 1, leading to overall growth and success.

Chapter 7

Technology

It was almost 11:00 PM And the team had gone home quite some time back. Only the 2 passionate people remained, talking about their way to march ahead.

“Feeling Sleepy? Should we call it a day?” Asked Aman. “Anyway, you had a long tiring day from your journey today”

“Not at all. This is by far the most interesting piece of research that I have ever come across. I could never have found this anywhere across any platform. Please continue” said Jayant with brightness in his eyes.

“Cool then. Let me order 2 cups of tea from Zomato and then we can continue with the second part.” said Aman.

While having a sip of tea, Aman asked Jayant

”Do you know the total number of tools you need to successfully climb Everest? And do you know the importance of each tool?”

“No” said Jayant unsurprisingly

"These are the total items required to climb Everest. And the best part is that every tool has its own significance" said Aman.

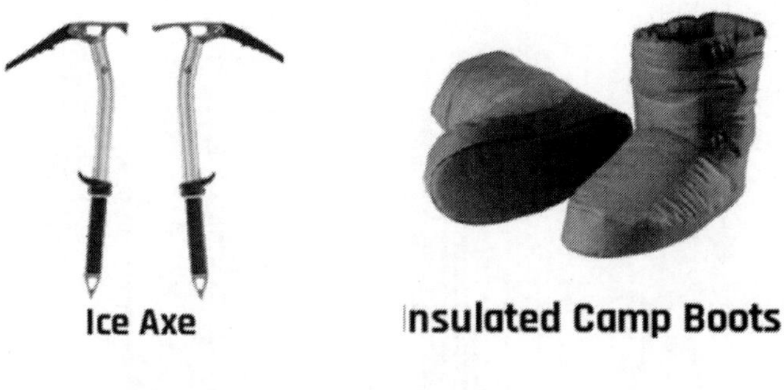

"Now if I ask you to climb Everest with just these 4 tools as shown in the figure above, will it be possible for you to reach the top?" asked Aman.

Mountaineering Gloves

"I would not even manage to reach halfway," said Jayant.

"Exactly, my dear friend, how do you believe that incorporating technology products like a Smartboard or a DSLR or a mic will help you sustain in an online platform easily?" asked Aman with a heavy voice.

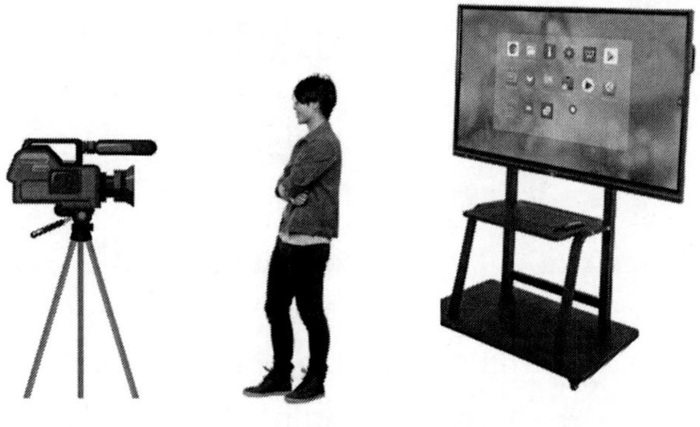

Jayant was speechless. He never saw this coming. He asked inquisitively "If not this then what? What am I missing?"

"Patience my friend," said Aman smilingly.

"There are 7 parameters a tech master online educator must be aware of" said Aman.

Let me explain:

1) 10-steps to keep in mind while selecting a perfect Smartboard (Interactive flat panel) for ou:

a. **Display Size:** Determine the appropriate display size based on the viewing distance in the classroom and based on the student's strength. For up to 40 offline students, I would suggest a 65" smart board. For 40 to 80 students' strength, a 75" smart board would be ideal, and for 80 and above student strength, an 86" smart board is suggested. For teaching online, the most suitable size is 75" because it is the perfect balance between pricing and providing an optimal viewing experience for online students.

b. **Touch Technology:** Look for panels with responsive and accurate touch technology, such as capacitive touch or infrared touch. My suggestion is to always feel the touch response physically before finalizing your choice because there can be discrepancies between what you see online and the actual touch experience.

c. **Play Store:** In my opinion, if the RAM of an Android 11 based Smartboard is only 4GB then having a play store is of no use because if you install any application it will hang the board very frequently. Play Store is recommended for 8 or 16 GB RAM in the Android version.

d. **OPS:** If you are an educator who works on PPT, having an OPS-based IFP is a must. OPS allows you to run Windows 10 or 11 on it. In the Windows interface, MS Office can be easily installed but you cannot find MS Office in the Android based panel nor can you install it. OPS allows you to store more content and resources for your presentation as it offers a minimum 128GB. While purchasing it, ensure to inquire the seller if they are giving the OPS and the panel of the same brand. You need to be careful of the things you do not know and it is my responsibility to inform you about these considerations.

e. **Software:** MS Office 2021 is indeed a best choice for educators as it allows users to save annotated and scribbled content for a lifetime. Apart from this Note 3 is widely popular because of its extensive functionality, providing resources and tools that cater the needs of JEE aspirants. Moreover, WhatsApp can be used as an application in some of the smart boards.

f. **Durability and Quality:** It is essential to pay attention to the build quality and durability of the panel, especially if it will be frequently used in a classroom. Foreign brands generally excel in durability when compared to Indian brands. Also, the display & touch quality of foreign brands is much better than display & touch quality of Indian brands. If you use board for 6 to 7 hours daily and budget is not an issue consider a quality product because smart board is a long term investment.

g. **Delivery & payment:** The smart board is delivered from a central warehouse that is in some other location. For your benefit, you must always hold 20%-25% of the payment because of the following reasons.

   i. **Delay in delivery.** When a seller receives full payment, they often become relaxed which is a headache for an educator who has planned his classes based on the expected delivery.

   ii. **Used or duplicate product delivered.** You are likely aware of the scams happening in online selling nowadays where what you see is not always what you get. Always keep some money in your hand which should be given only after you are satisfied with the quality of product or service received.

h. **Service:** As an educator, this is the most important point for you. If anything major happens to your smart board, you would be at risk as it can disrupt your classes, your investment is at stake, and much more. From a service perspective, always select a seller who has their own service team because, in the first place, you will contact the seller and not any company service center. Here the seller should be able to support you by sending his team member directly to assist you. It is also advisable to seek out an authorized dealer of a brand.

i. **Stand-by support:** In case of any major issue, always request for a stand-by support/stand-by panel. Since the panels are not typically repaired on-site, it usually takes weeks to get them repaired even under warranty. Hence during that time, you should have a spare panel on which you can take classes. It can be free or paid depending on the policy.

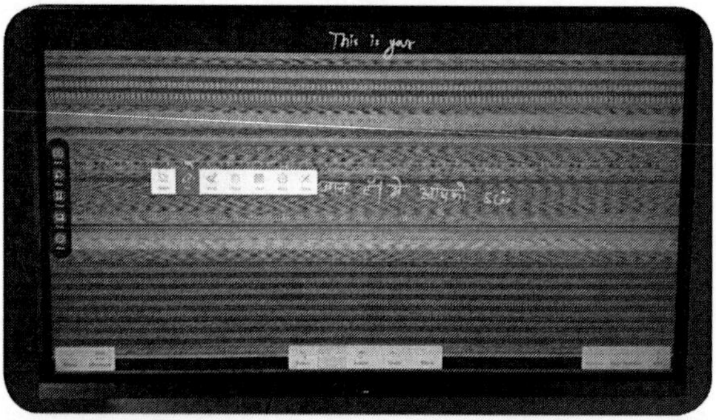

j. **Budget:** Consider your budget constraints and strive to strike a balance between features and affordability. Compare multiple models and brands to find the best value for your specific requirements.

2) Camera Flickering control mechanism

With the camera, you can observe facial expressions, gestures, and body language, thereby enhancing understanding. The camera adds a human element to online classes, making the learning experience more interactive and personal. However, as an educator, certain mistakes are made when choosing a camera. You must ensure there is no flickering in the panel. Flickering is the black and white lines as seen in the image.

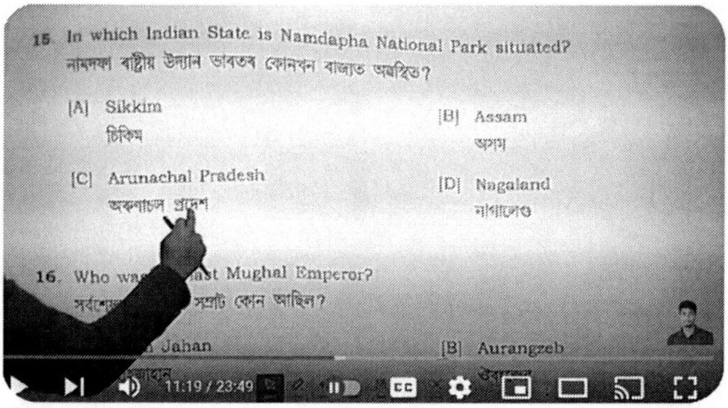

There are 2-3 mobile phones available that do not experience flickering and they also offer the capability to record your sessions. You can connect with me to learn more about these options. However, if you intend to go live, using a 4K PTZ camera is recommended. A mobile is a budget-friendly solution whereas a PTZ is a more professional solution.

Once the videos are recorded, they can be shared with students for a recap of concepts or can be uploaded on various online platforms such as YouTube or the Professional Android App.

3) The 3- oint lighting system

A bad lighting can do this to your video

The 3-point lighting system stands as the cornerstone of lighting when teaching online.

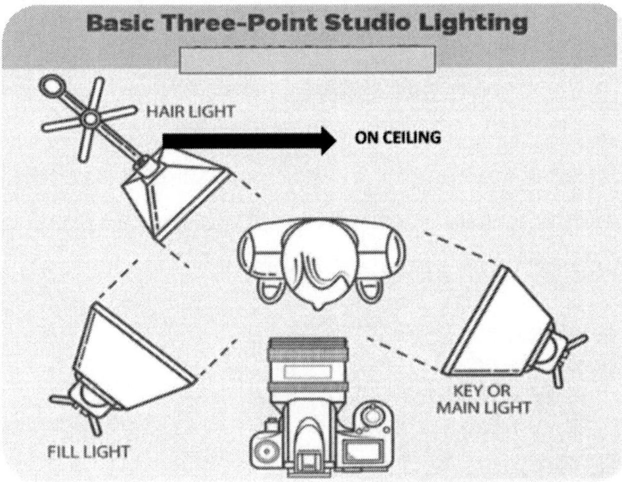

As shown in the figure above, three lights are present, one positioned on top and two on the sides. The top light, also known as the hair light, should be at least 200W or more and ideally positioned at a height of 5 to 6 ft above the teacher's head.

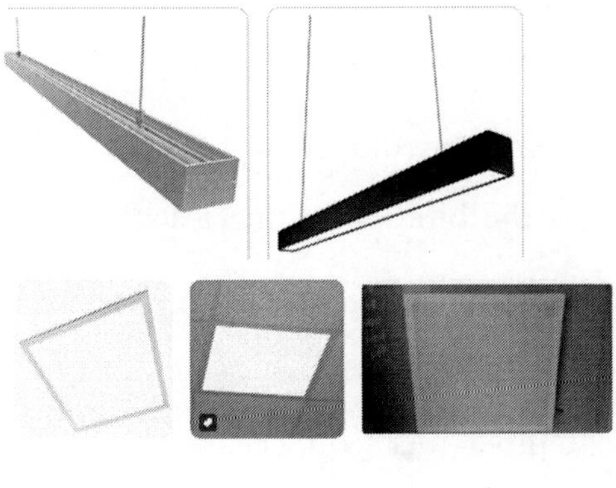

Side lights are mainly for the face to keep well-lit.. The power should be 100W on each side. These side lights can be in the form of tube lights or umbrella lights.

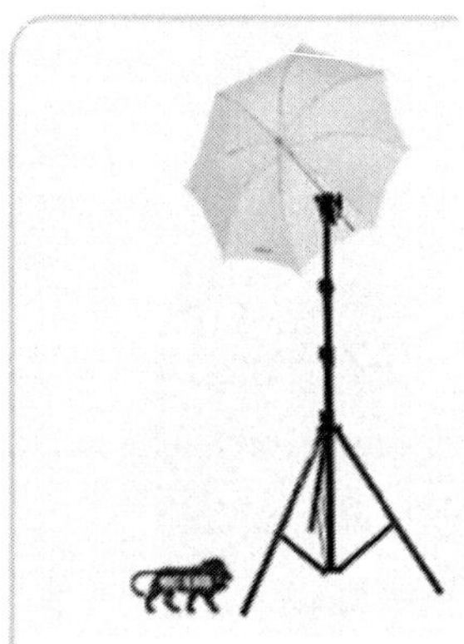

If you want you can throw a light from the bottom angle as well but it is not required.

4) Echo-controlling mechanism

This sequence is the bible of online teaching.

Your Audio > Your Content > Your Video editing > Your Lighting > Your Camera.

Always remember this sequence.

Whenever you make a video, ensure that the audio quality is the best. With poor audio, even great content is a flop.

There are 2 things that make good audio in a video. Mic and Soundproofing.

a) Mics:

The mics required for online sessions must have noise-cancellation techniques. There is a wide range of options available, ranging from 1200/- wireless mics to high-end 25000/- wireless mics. As an educator, 2000-3000 is the ideal price point where you can find a decent wireless noise cancellation mic available for purchase online.

b) Sound control:

As we all know sound is a wave, so in a large room a sound wave bounces and is returned in the form of an echo. The best practice is to have a room of 10x10 feet for online classes. You can paste thick foams on the wall whose main task is to absorb the reflected sound waves coming while speaking, otherwise all the sound will bounce back from the walls and hit back to the mic thus creating bad audio for listener.

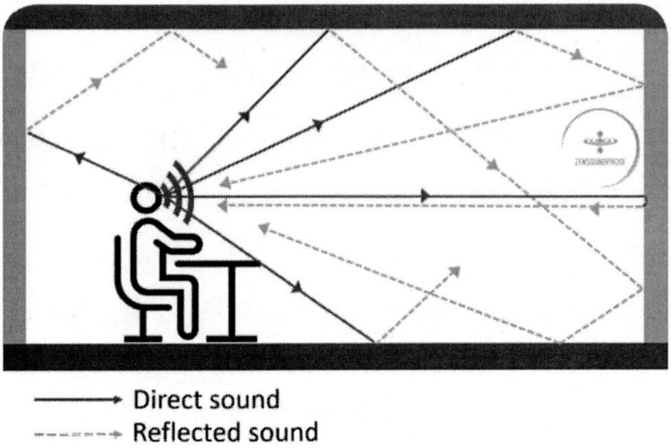

It is suggested that you seal all walls and balconies with thick plywood and make the room completely enclosed to prevent any external noise from entering the room.

5) Software knowledge for Professional Video Output

Educators should use OBS Studio software to enhance their teaching and create engaging educational content. OBS Studio (Open Broadcaster Software) is a free and open-source software for video recording and live streaming. Here are some ways educators can utilize OBS Studio:

Recording classes: Educators can use OBS Studio to record their classes or lectures. They can capture their computer screen, PTZ camera, and audio to create high-quality video content that can be shared with students later.

Live streaming: OBS Studio allows educators to live stream (eg: YT live) their classes or presentations. They can stream their screen, camera, or both simultaneously. Live streaming enables real-time interaction with students

Recording and streaming equipment: OBS Studio is compatible with various recording and streaming equipment, such as PTZ cameras, microphones, and other devices. Educators can enhance the audiovisual quality of their lessons by using external devices and configuring them with OBS Studio.

Video editing: Although OBS Studio primarily focuses on recording and streaming, it also provides basic video editing capabilities. Educators can trim recorded videos, add transitions, or make simple edits within the software itself before sharing the final content with students on YouTube or any other platform.

5) Power backup system

When taking any online class or offline class you need to ensure that you have a power backup in case of any power failure. Let us explore why

a. **Uninterrupted Teaching and Presentations:** Power failure can disrupt teaching sessions or presentations. However, by employing a power backup solution, such as an inverter or online UPS, the interactive flat panel can continue to operate even during power failures. This ensures that educators can seamlessly deliver their lessons or presentations without interruptions.

b. **Data Protection and Preservation:** Power interruptions can lead to data loss or corruption if the device shuts down unexpectedly. Having a power backup safeguards against data loss and preserves the integrity of valuable educational content stored on the interactive flat panel.

c. **Fighting Downtime:** Power disruptions can result in downtime while waiting for power to be restored or alternative arrangements to be made. This downtime can negatively impact teaching schedules. Already having the pressure to complete courses on time, having to wait for every time the power goes off, adds more pressure. By having a power backup, educators can seamlessly continue their teaching activities without disruptions or delays, minimizing any adverse effects on the learning process.

With the clock nearing 1 am, Aman concluded the session, confidently knowing that Jayant was now armed with the knowledge and enthusiasm to implement the *TT framework*. Jayant could not contain his excitement and expressed his gratitude to Aman for sharing his expertise and guiding him on this transformative journey.

Leaving Aman's office with renewed determination, Jayant felt inspired to apply the *TT framework* and embark on his online growth. He took a taxi to a nearby hotel but his mind buzzed with ideas and plans.

However, before leaving Jayant asked Aman one question.

"What if I get stuck in the journey? What if I have questions while implementing *TT Framework*? It seems nearly impossible to do it all on my own" said Jayant, expressing doubts swirling in his mind.

Aman smiled and said, "Don't worry!! Main hoon na" and then they went their own ways.

Chapter 8

Life after Implementing TT Framework

Today, thanks to the integration of innovative techniques and cutting-edge technology, he successfully tripled his student count, experiencing a substantial increase from 130 to 390 students.

The TT Framework revolutionized Jayant's teaching business as well as the learning experience for students. The blend of online and offline models brought a huge income to Jayant as his business grew by 4 times.

Jayant's phenomenal success story spread rapidly, igniting inspiration and influencing over 100 educators and policymakers to adopt the TT Framework in their institutions. As a result, Jayant and his institute emerged as the top pick for parents and students.

The success story of an educator has swiftly gone viral in just 2 years. While media houses have been keen to feature Jayant's story, he opts to remain low-key. On the other hand, with the increase in revenue, the Marketing budget has increased 10 times and Jayant now is planning to expand his coaching with his own application and bigger offline batch. Beyond teaching, his sole dedication is to mastermind effective marketing and innovative approaches.

Throughout the various scenarios presented earlier, there was one constant factor: Jayant's relentless commitment to putting in extra effort, even as his student base expanded threefold, and his proficiency in achieving results with the assistance of technology.

Conclusion

In conclusion, throughout this book, we delved into the powerful and transformative concept of the *TT Framework* – a combination of technique and technology that empowers educators to thrive in the hybrid teaching world. As we come to the end of this journey, let us recap the key insights and takeaways we have acquired.

First and foremost, we have explored the crucial role of technique in online growth.

Mastering the 4 steps of the technique is very important.

The ability to understand and connect with your target audience, create your videos to their needs, and consistently deliver value are all fundamental components of generating leads.

Your online foundation serves as the platform to attract students. Anything from Whatsapp App to LMS to your own coaching institute application works here. The choice depends on your funding capabilities.

Next, we create an online batch for basic/beginner level batch aiming to gather as many students as possible in this single batch while providing valuable content.

Last but not the least for a more advanced and student centric approach, create offline batches based on the demand generated from the online batch. Do not try to sell yourself. Let the students fight for a seat in your offline class.

Furthermore, you have acknowledged the significance of technology in facilitating your growth plans. The ever-evolving technological landscape offers you an array of powerful tools and platforms to leverage. These will also help you to make minimum errors while growing online.

In the end, the *TT Framework* provides you with a comprehensive framework for success in the digital age. By blending effective techniques with cutting-edge technology, you position to thrive amidst the leads of today and tomorrow.

May the knowledge and insights gained from this book serve as a catalyst for your ongoing journey toward growth and success. Embrace the power of the *TT Framework*, and may your endeavors be accompanied by endless possibilities and extraordinary achievements.

End

If you're an educator looking for assistance in the implementation of the *TT framework*, I encourage you to feel free to connect with me. I am here to provide support and guidance in incorporating the *TT framework* into your teaching practice. Whether you have questions, need suggestions, or require additional resources, don't hesitate to reach out. I am available to assist you in navigating the intricacies of the *TT framework* and help you make the most of this approach in your classroom. Let's work together to create a positive and effective learning environment for your students.

I eagerly look forward to hearing about your experiences and transformations resulting from the principles shared in this book. Your feedback is invaluable and will contribute to my ongoing work and future publications. Feel free to reach out with any questions or to delve deeper into these principles. Your thoughts, insights, and inquiries are highly valued and encouraged. You can connect with me directly at

atul.jain@swastiksystems.in

Feel free to connect with me for any help you may need in implementing the *TT framework.*

My best wishes!!

Atul Jain

Creator of TT Framework
The Ultimate Guidebook to a Successful Coaching Profession